Inside Animal Homes

Inside Beaver Lodges

Emily Wilson

PowerKiDS press.

New York

Published in 2016 by The Rosen Publishing Group, Inc.
29 East 21st Street, New York, NY 10010

First Edition

Editor: Sarah Machajewski
Book Design: Mickey Harmon

Photo Credits: Cover, pp. 1, 5 (beavers) Robert McGouey/Getty Images; cover, pp. 3–4, 6, 8, 10, 12, 14, 16, 18, 20, 22–24 (pond background) Beth Swanson/Shutterstock.com; cover, pp. 1, 3–4, 6, 8, 10, 12, 14, 16, 18, 20, 22–24 (magnifying glass shape) musicman/Shutterstock.com; p. 5 Henrik Larsson/Shutterstock.com; p. 7 Muskoka Stock Photos/Shutterstock.com; p. 9 (inset) Lee Rue III - Leonard/Getty Images; p. 9 (main) TOM MCHUGH/Getty Images; p. 11 Edward Kinsman/Getty Images; p. 13 (inset) Grambo Photography/Getty Images; p. 13 (main) Michael Giannechini/Getty Images; p. 15 Alan and Sandy Carey/Getty Images; p. 19 (upper) LesPalenik/Shutterstock.com; p. 19 (lower) © iStockphoto.com/Terryfic3D; p. 21 (main) Krzysztof Wiktor/Shutterstock.com; p. 21 (deer) Bruce MacQueen/Shutterstock.com; p. 21 (frog) Artur Synenko/Shutterstock.com; p. 21 (muskrat) Sergey Uryadnikov/Shutterstock.com; p. 21 (bear) Gail Johnson/Shutterstock.com; p. 21 (moose) Tony Campbell/Shutterstock.com; p. 21 (bird) asharkyu/Shutterstock.com; p. 22 Daniel Rose/Shutterstock.com.

Cataloging-in-Publication Data

Wilson, Emily.
Inside beaver lodges / by Emily Wilson.
p. cm. — (Inside animal homes)
Includes index.
ISBN 978-1-4994-0872-0 (pbk.)
ISBN 978-1-4994-0886-7 (6 pack)
ISBN 978-1-4994-0915-4 (library binding)
1. Beavers — Habitations — Juvenile literature. 2. Beavers — Juvenile literature. I. Wilson, Emily. II. Title.
QL737.R632 W557 2016
599.37—d23

Manufactured in the United States of America

CPSIA Compliance Information: Batch #WS15PK: For Further Information contact Rosen Publishing, New York, New York at 1-800-237-9932

Contents

Changing the Landscape

Beavers may be one of nature's busiest animals. They're born to build, and that's exactly what they do. Beavers spend their life cutting down trees and gathering sticks, branches, and mud. They use them to create homes called lodges.

Lodges do much more than give beavers a place to live. They often completely change the **landscape** where they're built. This affects all the surrounding plants and animals. Read on to discover why lodges—and the beavers that build them—are so important.

This pile of sticks may not look like much,
but it's a home for beavers!

5

Where Do Beavers Live?

Beavers are a kind of **mammal** called rodents. They're one of the largest rodents in the world. There are two species, or kinds, of beaver. They live in North America, Europe, and Asia. In North America, beavers can be found throughout Canada and the United States, except Florida and parts of California.

Beavers make their homes in forests. They live around rivers and streams. This kind of **environment** is perfect for beavers. It has plenty of water and trees for building homes.

THE INSIDE SCOOP

Beavers live in areas known as riparian zones. This name comes from a Latin word that means "river bank."

This forest is a perfect place for a beaver to live. In fact, beavers helped make the pond you see here.

Beaver Body

A beaver's body is perfect for the kind of environments it calls home. It has a round body and short legs. Its back legs and wide, flat tail help a beaver swim. A beaver's front feet have five claws. A beaver uses them to dig and carry branches.

If there's one thing a beaver is known for, it's having big front teeth. They're orange because they have iron instead of calcium like our teeth do, and they're always growing! These teeth are very sharp. They help a beaver cut down the trees it needs to build its home.

THE INSIDE SCOOP

Beaver fur is waterproof, or able to keep water out. This keeps a beaver's body warm and dry as it swims.

A beaver's teeth are always growing. Chewing through trees helps wear the teeth down so they don't get too long.

Choosing the Place

Beavers' homes play a very important part in their life. Building lodges is their most important job. Once they're built, lodges become a place to live, stay safe from predators, store food, and raise young.

The first step in constructing a beaver lodge is to pick a place to build it. Beavers always choose areas with streams or rivers for their home. However, once they're done building, the landscape will look completely different. It may even create a brand-new **ecosystem**.

This photo shows how a beaver lodge can change the surrounding area. Land that was once covered with dirt and plants is slowly turning into a pond.

Building Dams

Lodges keep beavers safe from predators. In order to **protect** their lodge, beavers first build a **structure** called a dam. A dam is a **barrier** of branches and mud built across a river or stream. It stops the flow of water and creates a pond behind it.

Water backs up behind the dam and creates a big pool of sitting water. Lodges are built in the middle of the pool. Soon, no one but beavers can reach it. If beavers sense danger near the lodge, they slap the water with their tail. The tail slap warns other beavers of danger.

THE INSIDE SCOOP

Scientists have discovered that the sound and feel of running water makes beavers want to build dams.

A beaver sends out a warning signal.

lodge

dam

Beavers build their lodge upstream from their dam.

Starting Construction

Beavers are hard workers. They cut down trees with their sharp teeth. Once they start chewing, they don't stop until the job is done. If a log is too big to carry, they cut it into smaller pieces. Beavers also gather twigs and branches from the ground. They lay these **materials** in a pile in the middle of the water.

Next, beavers fill in the open spaces with stones and leaves. Then, using their feet, they spread mud all over the lodge. This keeps water from getting inside.

THE INSIDE SCOOP

Beavers carry branches with their teeth as they swim. Their lips close behind their big front teeth, keeping water out of their mouth.

Beavers build their homes during spring and summer so they have a warm, dry place for the winter.

Going Inside

Beavers are smart! They build special features that make their lodge a safe and dry place to live. They build entrances underwater. Predators can't see them, which means they can't get in. These entrances lead to tunnels. The tunnels meet in the center of the lodge, which is a big **chamber**.

A small hole, or vent, in the roof of the lodge lets in fresh air. Beavers store piles of food underwater, just outside the entrances. During winter, they can easily swim in and out to grab it.

THE INSIDE SCOOP

Beavers eat tree bark and certain kinds of plants. They store food so they have it to eat when the water freezes over and they can't leave the pond.

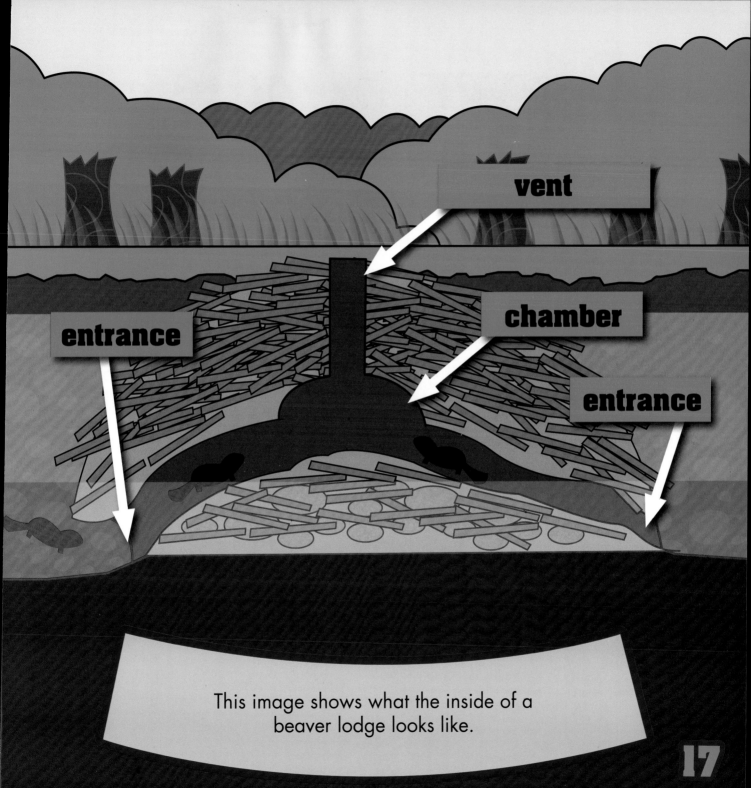

vent

chamber

entrance

entrance

This image shows what the inside of a beaver lodge looks like.

Beaver Families

Though beavers must enter and leave the lodge underwater, the lodge itself is above water. The inside chamber stays warm and dry all winter long.

Beaver families are called colonies. The whole colony lives together in the lodge. A colony has an adult male and an adult female. They remain a pair for life. Colonies also have beaver babies, which are called kits, and yearlings, which are one-year-old beavers. Young beavers leave the colony when they're about two years old.

THE INSIDE SCOOP

Beaver lodges have anywhere from 6 to 10 beavers living in them at a time.

A beaver lodge is the perfect place to be in winter. It's warm, dry, and safe. Kits, such as the one pictured here, are born inside lodges during winter.

Ecosystem Engineers

Beavers are often called "nature's **engineers**" because of how their building changes the landscape. Their construction changes the way the environment looks, but it also shapes ecosystems.

Making dams creates ponds, which gives plants, bugs, and animals a home. Trees beavers cut down but don't use become homes for birds and other small mammals. These creatures become sources of food for other animals. Soon, a beaver pond is busy with the activity of a brand-new ecosystem.

These are just some of the creatures that are part of the ecosystems beavers create.

frogs

muskrats

moose

birds

bears

deer

21

Protect the Beaver

The amazing beaver can do a lot to change the environment. While this is good in wild areas, it can create problems when it happens too close to people. Beavers sometimes chew down trees in people's yards. Building dams close to roads may cause them to flood. If this happens, it's important to not hurt beavers. They're just doing what they do best: building homes!

The next time you see a pile of sticks in water, look closer. Could there be a home inside?

Glossary

barrier: Something that stops movement.

chamber: A room.

ecosystem: All the living things in an area.

engineer: Someone who is a skillful planner and builder.

environment: The conditions that surround a living thing and affect the way it lives.

landscape: The landforms of an area.

mammal: A warm-blooded animal that has a backbone and hair, breathes air, and feeds milk to its young.

material: Matter that can be used to make something.

protect: To keep safe.

structure: A building or other object constructed of several parts.

Index

B
babies, 18
branches, 4, 8,
     12, 14

C
chamber, 16, 17, 18
colonies, 18

D
dam, 12, 13, 20, 22

E
ecosystem, 10, 20
entrances, 16, 17

F
feet, 8, 14
fur, 8

K
kits, 18, 19

L
legs, 8

M
mammal, 6, 20
mud, 4, 12, 14

P
pond, 7, 11, 12,
     16, 20
predators, 10, 12, 16

R
rivers, 6, 10, 12

S
species, 6
sticks, 4, 5, 22
stream, 6, 10,
     12, 13

T
tail, 8, 12
teeth, 8, 9, 14
trees, 4, 6, 8, 9, 14,
     16, 20, 22
tunnels, 16

V
vent, 16, 17

W
water, 6, 8, 12,
     14, 16, 18, 22

Websites

Due to the changing nature of Internet links, PowerKids Press has developed an online list of websites related to the subject of this book. This site is updated regularly. Please use this link to access the list: www.powerkidslinks.com/home/beav